MW00954363

NATURAL DISASTERS

A Collection of Inspiring Survival Stories about Friendship, Courage, and Rescue to Motivate Young Minds

MICHELLE BURTON
2025

Inspiring Survival Stories for Kids

WHAT'S INSIDE?

ABOUT THE AUTHOR

 **Michelle Burton** has a special gift for turning everyday wonders into captivating stories that spark the imagination and curiosity of young readers. As the happy mother of two curious kids, Michelle draws inspiration from her own children's questions, always striving to answer their "whys" and "hows" in the most captivating ways possible.

From a young age, Michelle was enchanted by the power of books. She would spend hours lost in stories, exploring distant lands, and learning about incredible facts. This early passion for reading led her to become an elementary school teacher, where she found joy in sharing the magic of learning with her students. Watching their eyes light up with curiosity and excitement inspired her to start writing her books.

Her goal is to turn every child who reads her books into a curious explorer of the world around him. Michelle believes that learning doesn't stop in the classroom - it's a lifelong journey that can happen anywhere and anytime.

In this book, Michelle Burton invites young readers to embark on a journey of discovery. She hopes this book will not only answer some of the most intriguing questions but also inspire children to ask their own and seek out the incredible knowledge that the world has to offer.

Chapter 1: INTRODUCTION TO SURVIVAL STORIES

Throughout history, people have faced incredible challenges when nature shows its most powerful side. From earthquakes that shake entire cities to hurricanes that bring fierce winds and rain, natural disasters can be terrifying. But in these moments of danger, there are also stories of bravery, friendship, and the unbreakable human spirit.

Natural Disasters is a collection of true stories about people, who faced some of the most dangerous forces on Earth — and survived! These stories are not only amazing because of the disasters, but because of the courage, quick thinking, and teamwork that helped people overcome impossible odds.

In this book, you'll meet everyday heroes: children, families, and communities who found strength in each other. From the brave boy who saved his brother during a flood to the young girl who led her village to safety before a tsunami, these tales will inspire you and show that even in the toughest times, hope and resilience can shine through.

As you read these stories, you'll learn valuable lessons about staying calm, working together, and never giving up. Whether it's escaping the rush of an avalanche or surviving a massive earthquake, these survivors remind us that courage can come from anyone — no matter how young or old you are.

FOR PARENTS

Dear Parents,

as our children grow and explore the world around them, they will inevitably encounter stories about the forces of nature. Natural disasters — whether it's a hurricane, earthquake, tsunami, or flood — can be both awe-inspiring and frightening. It is important that our children not only understand the power of nature but also learn
how to find hope, courage, and strength in the face of such events.

Natural Disasters is more than just a collection of survival stories; it is a book designed to inspire young minds through real-life examples of bravery, resilience, and teamwork. Through these pages, your child will meet survivors who rely on their knowledge, instincts, and the support of others to overcome adversity. Whether it's a young boy guiding his family to safety during a tsunami or a group of friends rescuing each other during an avalanche, the stories emphasize the importance of staying calm and focused in the face of fear.

We've crafted the language and tone of this book to be accessible for children while ensuring that the key messages of courage and survival come through clearly. As parents, you can use these stories as opportunities to discuss safety preparedness and the importance of community and compassion during times of crisis.

We hope Fascinating Survivals from Natural Disasters will not only captivate your child's imagination but also equip them with a sense of empowerment — that even in the most challenging circumstances, hope, courage, and cooperation can help us survive and thrive.

Sincerely,

Michelle Burton

FREE BONUS FOR YOU

As a special thank you for your purchase, we're thrilled to offer you a **FREE digital** "True or False Quiz about Science and Experiments". Enjoy over 20 **exciting physics and chemistry experiments** using everyday household items!

How to Get Your Gift:

Leave a review on this book on http://www.amazon.com sharing your thoughts about this book.

 Positive ratings, reviews, and suggestions from interested people like you help others to feel confident about choosing this book and help us provide great books.

Receive your exclusive "**True or False Quiz with Interesting Home Science Experiments**" absolutely **FREE**. Use a link below or a QR Code:

https://BookHip.com/NJWFVBD

THANK YOU IN ADVANCE FOR YOUR REVIEW!

2.1 What's an Earthquake?

An earthquake is when the ground shakes suddenly. This shaking happens because the Earth's crust (the outer layer of the Earth) moves. Let's find out more in a way that's easy to understand:

Why Do Earthquakes Happen?

o Tectonic Plates: Imagine the Earth's crust is like a big puzzle made of many pieces called tectonic plates. These plates fit together and cover the whole Earth.

o Moving Plates: These plates are always slowly moving, but sometimes they get stuck because of the rocks' rough edges.

o Release of Energy: When the plates finally get unstuck, they move quickly, releasing a lot of energy. This energy makes the ground shake, and that's what we feel as an earthquake.

What Happens During an Earthquake?

• Shaking Ground: During an earthquake, the ground shakes and moves. Sometimes the shaking is gentle, but other times it can be very strong.

• Waves: The energy from the earthquake moves through the ground in waves. These waves can travel a long way, making the ground shake in places far from where the earthquake started.

- Aftershocks: After the main earthquake, there are often smaller earthquakes called aftershocks. These can happen minutes, hours, or even days later.

Effects of an Earthquake

Buildings and Roads: Strong earthquakes can damage buildings, roads, and bridges. Sometimes, buildings can even collapse if the earthquake is very powerful.

Landslides: In hilly or mountainous areas, the shaking can cause landslides, where rocks and soil slide down the slopes.

Tsunamis: If an earthquake happens under the ocean, it can cause a tsunami, which is a series of big waves that can flood coastal areas.

How Can We Stay Safe During an Earthquake?

- Drop, Cover, and Hold On: If you feel the ground shaking, drop to your hands and knees, cover your head and neck with your arms, and hold on to something sturdy until the shaking stops.

- Stay Indoors: If you're inside, stay there and find a safe spot away from windows. If you're outside, move to an open area away from buildings, trees, and power lines.

- Emergency Kit: Having a kit with water, food, and other essentials can help you stay safe after an earthquake if you need to wait for help.

2.2 The Haiti Earthquake (2010): Resilience of the People

A Normal Day in Haiti

On January 12, 2010, the people of Haiti were going about their daily lives. Children were playing, parents were working, and everyone was enjoying the sunny weather. Haiti, a beautiful Caribbean country, was full of vibrant culture and friendly people.

The Earthquake Strikes

Suddenly, in the afternoon, the ground started to shake violently. It was a massive earthquake, measuring 7.0 on the Richter scale. Buildings began to crumble, roads cracked open, and homes were destroyed. The earthquake caused significant destruction, and many people were hurt or trapped.

Acts of Courage

Despite the fear and chaos, the people of Haiti showed incredible courage. Neighbors helped each other out of the rubble, and strangers became friends as they worked together to rescue those who were trapped. One brave boy named Jacques saw that his friend Marie was stuck under some fallen bricks. Without thinking about his own safety, Jacques rushed to help her. He carefully removed the bricks and pulled her to safety.

The Strength of the Community

In the days following the earthquake, the resilience of the Haitian people was truly inspiring. They worked together to find food, water, and shelter. Communities set up makeshift camps where they could stay safe. Even though they had lost so much, they shared what little they had with each other.

A woman named Alina, whose home was destroyed, set up a small kitchen in the camp. She cooked meals for everyone, using the food that people brought to her. Alina's kindness and determination helped keep spirits up and showed how powerful hope and solidarity could be.

Rebuilding Lives

Rescue teams and aid workers from around the world came

to help the people of Haiti. They brought medical supplies, food, and clean water. The Haitian people welcomed them and worked alongside them to rebuild their communities.

Jacques and his friend Marie, along with other children, helped clean up the debris and build new shelters. They worked hard, knowing that every bit of effort made a difference. Their smiles and laughter brought hope to everyone around them.

A New Beginning

Slowly but surely, the people of Haiti began to rebuild their lives. Schools were reopened, and children went back to learning and playing. New homes were built, stronger and safer than before. The spirit of the Haitian people, their resilience and strength, shone through as they created a new beginning for themselves and their communities.

A Lesson in Courage and Resilience

The story of the Haiti earthquake teaches us about the incredible courage and resilience of the Haitian people. Even in the face of great tragedy, they showed the power of hope and the importance of helping one another. Their determination to rebuild their lives and support each other is a powerful example of how strong and caring people can be.

For young readers, this story reminds us that even when things seem very difficult, we can find strength in ourselves and in our communities. By working together and staying hopeful, we can overcome challenges and create a better future.

2.3 The Langtang Valley Rescue in Nepal

A Journey to the Mountains

In April 2015, a group of friends went on a trekking adventure to Langtang Valley in Nepal. The group included Lily, a friendly guide who knew the mountains well; Sam, an adventurous boy who loved exploring; Maya, a girl who enjoyed taking pictures of nature; and Raju, a boy who loved learning about new places and people.

Langtang Valley was beautiful, with tall mountains, green forests, and traditional villages. The friends were excited to see the

snow-capped peaks and learn about the culture of the people living there.

The Earthquake Strikes

On April 25, the ground suddenly shook as they walked through the valley. At 11:56 a.m. that day, a 7.8-magnitude earthquake shook Nepal. It was a powerful earthquake! The mountains rumbled, and snow started sliding down the slopes, creating loud, booming noises. The ground beneath their feet began to shake violently. The shaking was so strong that it made it hard to stand up. The friends were scared, but they knew they had to find a safe place quickly.

Lily, the guide, remembered a nearby teahouse, a type of mountain lodge that trekkers and locals often used for rest. "Follow me, everyone!" Lily called out, her voice steady despite the fear they all felt.

The group ran after Lily, dodging small rocks and snow falling from the slopes. The teahouse was not far, but the shaking ground made every step challenging. The mountains' loud rumbling and the avalanches' crashing sounds were terrifying, but they focused on reaching the shelter.

Finding Safety Together

The teahouse was a small but strong building made from thick stone walls. These walls were built to handle the tough conditions of the mountains, including heavy snow and cold winds. Lily knew that such a building would also provide good protection during an earthquake because the stones were heavy and firmly in place.

As they approached the teahouse, Lily reassured her friends, "This building is very strong. It's one of the safest places we can be right now." Her calm confidence helped to soothe their nerves. The building shook, and everyone could hear the distant sounds of avalanches. Despite the fear, they were relieved to be in a safe place.

Sam noticed they had only a little food and water. Maya suggested they share what they had and make it last as long as possible. Everyone agreed, so they carefully rationed their food, making sure everyone had enough to eat each day.

Staying Calm and Helping Each Other

Lily kept everyone calm, explaining that rescue teams would come as soon as they could. She showed them how to collect snow to melt for water and made sure everyone stayed warm. Maya, with her camera, took pictures to document their experience, helping to keep everyone's spirits up by focusing on the beauty around them.

Raju organized games and told stories to keep everyone entertained. He knew staying positive and engaged was important to keep their minds off the outside danger. The friends supported each other, sharing warmth and encouraging words.

The Rescue

After several days, the group heard the sound of helicopters. They were filled with hope! They used colorful clothing and shiny objects to signal the rescue teams. Soon, helicopters began landing near the teahouse, bringing rescuers to help them.

The rescue teams worked hard to bring everyone to safety. The friends were airlifted to a safe area where they received food, water, and medical care. They were grateful and relieved, knowing they had made it through a very difficult situation together.

A Lesson in Friendship and Calm

The story of the Langtang Valley rescue teaches us about the importance of staying calm, working together, and supporting each other in tough times. The friends showed how staying positive and using their skills helped them survive a natural disaster. Their experience reminds us that even in scary situations, we can find strength in friendship and teamwork.

For young readers, this story shows that by staying calm and helping one another, we can overcome challenges and find hope, even in the most difficult times.

2.4 The 1985 Mexico City Earthquake: The Miracle of the Babies

A Busy Morning in Mexico City

On the morning of September 19, 1985, Mexico City was bustling with activity. People were heading to work, children were getting ready for school, and the city was full of life. It was a typical busy day in one of the largest cities in the world.

The Earthquake Strikes

At 7:19 AM, everything changed. A massive earthquake shook the city with incredible force. Buildings swayed and collapsed, roads cracked open, and there was dust and debris everywhere. The earthquake was very strong, causing a lot of damage and leaving many people trapped under the rubble.

The Rescue Efforts Begin

Rescue teams and volunteers from all over the city rushed to help. They worked tirelessly to save people trapped in the collapsed buildings. Among the rubble was a hospital where many babies had just been born. The building had collapsed, and everyone feared the worst.

The Miracle Babies

Days passed, and the rescue workers continued their efforts, not giving up hope. On the fourth day, something amazing happened. As the rescuers were digging through the rubble of the hospital, they heard faint cries. They carefully moved the debris and found several newborn babies alive!

These babies had survived for days without food or water, and their discovery brought immense joy and hope to everyone.

The rescuers named them "The Miracle Babies" because their survival was so incredible. The tiny infants were quickly taken to another hospital where they received the care they needed.

Their survival was a beacon of hope amid the tragedy.

A Community United

The discovery of the Miracle Babies inspired the rescue workers and the entire community. People came together to support each other, sharing food, water, and shelter. Volunteers worked side by side with professionals, showing incredible courage and determination.

One of the rescue workers, Carlos, said, "Finding those babies alive gave us the strength to keep going. It reminded us that even in the darkest times, there is always hope."

2.5 The 1995 Kobe Earthquake: The Spirit of Gaman

A Normal Morning in Kobe

On January 17, 1995, the city of Kobe in Japan started out just like any other day. People were waking up, getting ready for work and school, and going about their usual routines. The streets were busy, and everything seemed normal.

The Earthquake Strikes

Suddenly, at 5:46 AM, the ground began to shake violently. It was a powerful earthquake, later measured at 7.2 on the Richter scale. Buildings swayed, roads cracked, and houses collapsed. The earthquake caused widespread destruction in Kobe and the surrounding areas. People were thrown from their beds, and many buildings were damaged or destroyed.

The Immediate Aftermath

Amidst the chaos, people were scared and unsure of what to do. However, in the midst of this disaster, something incredible happened. The people of Kobe showed an amazing spirit of "gaman," a Japanese word that means patience and perseverance.

Patience and Perseverance

Gaman is a very important concept in Japanese culture. It means to endure difficult situations with patience, without complaining, and to stay strong. The survivors of the Kobe earthquake showed gaman in many ways.

Neighbors helped each other out of the rubble, sharing food and water with those in need. Despite their own losses, people remained calm and supportive. They waited patiently for help to arrive, knowing that rescue teams were doing their best to reach everyone.

Acts of Courage

One story of courage involved a young boy named Kenji. When the earthquake struck, Kenji's house collapsed, trapping his family inside. Kenji was scared, but he remembered his father's advice to stay calm in emergencies.

Kenji crawled through the debris and found a way out. Instead of running to safety alone, he went to get help for his family. He found some neighbors who were already helping others and brought them back to his house. Together, they rescued Kenji's family from the rubble.

Helping Each Other

Throughout the city, people showed amazing acts of kindness and bravery. Schools and community centers became shelters for those who lost their homes. Volunteers distributed food, water, and blankets to keep everyone warm and fed. Even though they were scared and had lost so much, the people of Kobe supported each other with strength and patience.

The Spirit of Gaman

The spirit of gaman helped the community stay strong. Instead of giving up or losing hope, they worked together to rebuild their city. The patience and perseverance they showed made a big difference in the recovery process.

The Road to Recovery

The road to recovery was long and challenging. It took time to rebuild homes, schools, and businesses. But the people of Kobe never gave up. They showed great courage and determination, and slowly, their city began to heal.

Kenji and his family, like many others, found a new home and started rebuilding their lives. The support from neighbors, friends, and even strangers helped them overcome the difficulties they faced.

A Lesson in Courage

The story of the 1995 Kobe earthquake teaches us about the importance of patience, perseverance, and helping each other. The spirit of gaman helped the people of Kobe stay strong during one of the toughest times in their lives. It shows that even in the face of great challenges, we can find strength in ourselves and in our community.

For young readers, this story reminds us that courage isn't just about being brave; it's also about being patient, staying positive, and supporting those around us. The people of Kobe showed us that by working together and never giving up, we can overcome any obstacle.

3.1 What's a Tsunami?

A tsunami is a big, powerful wave that comes from the ocean and can cause a lot of damage when it reaches the shore. Here's an easy way to understand what happens:

How Does a Tsunami Start?

- Earthquakes: Sometimes, the ground under the ocean shakes a lot. This shaking happens because the Earth's crust (the outer layer of the Earth) moves around. When the crust moves suddenly, it can push a lot of water fast, creating huge waves.

- Volcanoes: There are also volcanoes under the ocean. When they erupt, they can push water out of the way and make big waves too.

- Landslides: Sometimes, big pieces of land fall into the ocean. This can happen underwater or from the edge of the land into the sea. When this happens, it pushes the water and makes waves.

What Happens When a Tsunami Comes?

Speed: Tsunamis move very fast in the deep ocean, like a jet plane flying in the sky. But you might not even see them because the waves are not very high out in the deep water.

Waves Get Bigger: As the tsunami gets closer to the shore, the water becomes shallower. The waves slow down and get much taller. This is when they can become very dangerous.

Series of Waves: A tsunami isn't just one wave. It's a series of waves that can come one after another. The time between these waves can be a few minutes or even over an hour.

What Can Tsunamis Do?

- Flooding: When these huge waves reach the land, they can flood coastal areas. This means water covers places where people live, work, and play.

- Strong Currents: The water can move very fast and push things like cars, houses, and trees. It can be very dangerous for people and animals.

- Damage: Tsunamis can break buildings, roads, and other things people use every day. They can also change the shape of the coastlines.

How Can We Stay Safe?

Warning Systems: Scientists have special tools to detect tsunamis early. They can send warnings to people living near the coast to move to higher ground. **Evacuation Plans:** Many places have plans to help people know what to do if a tsunami is coming. Practicing these plans can help keep everyone safe.

Remember:

A tsunami is a big and powerful wave caused by movements under the ocean. They can be very dangerous, but with the right knowledge and preparation, we can stay safe. Always listen to warnings and follow safety instructions if you live near the coast.

3.2 The Story of Tilly Smith (2004)

A Family Vacation in Thailand

During the winter holidays in 2004, a 10-year-old girl named Tilly Smith was on vacation with her family in Thailand. They were staying at a beautiful beach resort, enjoying the sunny weather, the sandy beaches, and the warm ocean water. Tilly loved exploring the beach and playing in the waves with her younger sister.

A Fun Day at the Beach

On the morning of December 26, Tilly and her family decided to spend the day at the beach. The sky was clear, and the sun was shining brightly. Families were relaxing on the sand, children were building sandcastles, and everyone was having a wonderful time. But something caught Tilly's attention.

As she looked out at the ocean, she noticed that the water was behaving strangely. The waves were receding far back, exposing the seabed, and small bubbles were forming on the surface. Tilly remembered learning about tsunamis in her geography lessons at school. She recalled her teacher explaining that these were signs of an approaching tsunami.

Recognizing the Danger

Tilly felt a surge of fear and urgency. She knew she had to act quickly to save her family and others on the beach. "Mom, Dad, we have to get off the beach! There's going to be a tsunami!" she shouted, her voice filled with alarm.

At first, her parents were confused. They looked around and saw that everyone else seemed calm. But Tilly insisted, "I learned about this in school! When the sea pulls back like that, it means a big wave is coming!"

Alerting Others

Tilly's parents trusted her and decided to take her warning

seriously. They quickly gathered their belongings and started to move away from the beach. As they did, Tilly's father began to warn others, shouting, "There's a tsunami coming! We need to get to higher ground!"

The people on the beach were startled, but seeing the urgency in Tilly's father's actions, many began to follow suit. Some hesitated, not fully understanding the danger, but Tilly continued to urge everyone to move quickly.

Reaching Safety

Tilly and her family, along with many other tourists and locals, ran towards the higher ground near their hotel. They climbed up a hill, away from the beach, and found a safe spot to wait. Tilly's heart was pounding, but she felt a bit of relief knowing they had reached safety.

Moments later, they heard a loud roar. A massive wave crashed onto the beach, sweeping away everything in its path—beach chairs, umbrellas, and even small boats. The water surged inland, flooding the area where they had been just moments before.

The Aftermath

The tsunami caused widespread devastation in many coastal areas around the Indian Ocean, but thanks to Tilly's quick thinking and courage, many lives were saved that day on the beach in Thailand. Her awareness of the warning signs and her bravery in speaking up made a huge difference.

A Lesson in Courage and Awareness

Tilly's story teaches us the importance of education and being aware of our surroundings. Her knowledge from geography class helped her recognize the danger and act quickly to save lives. It shows that even young children can be heroes when they stay calm and use what they've learned.

For young readers, Tilly's story is a reminder that being brave and informed can help us protect ourselves and others in dangerous situations. It encourages everyone to pay attention in school and learn about safety because you never know when that knowledge might come in handy.

Tilly's courage and quick thinking during the 2004 tsunami are an inspiring example of how one person's actions can make a big difference, highlighting the power of education and the importance of staying calm in emergencies.

3.3 The 2004 Indian Ocean Tsunami: The Power of the Moken People

The Sea Nomads

The Moken people are known as sea nomads. They live in small villages on the islands and coasts of Thailand and Myanmar, and they spend much of their lives on the sea, fishing and diving. The Moken have a deep understanding and respect for nature. They learn from a young age to read the signs of the ocean and the weather.

A Beautiful Day Turns Dangerous

On December 26, 2004, it was a beautiful, sunny day. The Moken people were going about their daily activities. Children were playing on the beach, and the adults were preparing their boats for fishing. Everything seemed peaceful and normal.

The Warning Signs

Suddenly, some of the Moken elders noticed strange things happening. The sea started to recede far from the shore, exposing the seabed. Fish were flopping on the sand, and the water seemed unusually still. The Moken people had seen these signs before in their stories and teachings.

An elder named Laila remembered her grandfather's tales about the "laboon," which means "the wave that eats people." She knew that when the sea pulls back like this, a giant wave, a tsunami, is coming. She quickly warned everyone, "We need to move to higher ground now! A big wave is coming!"

Moving to Safety

The Moken people listened to Laila's warning. They trusted her wisdom and quickly began to move to higher ground. Parents grabbed their children, and everyone hurried away from the beach. They climbed up to the nearby hills, far from the shore.

The Tsunami Hits

Just minutes later, a massive tsunami wave crashed onto the shore, destroying everything in its path. The powerful wave swept away houses, boats, and trees. But thanks to Laila's quick thinking and the Moken's knowledge of nature, they were safe on the high ground.

The Moken people watched from the hills as the waves continued to surge and destroy their village. It was a devastating sight, but they were grateful to be alive and together.

The Aftermath

After the tsunami passed, the Moken people came down from the hills to see the damage. Their village was gone, and they had lost many of their belongings. But the most important thing was that they had survived. Their traditional knowledge and respect for nature had saved their lives.

The Moken community worked together to rebuild their homes and lives. They showed incredible strength and resilience, helping each other through the difficult times. They knew that their wisdom and connection to nature were powerful tools for survival.

A Lesson in Courage and Wisdom

The story of the Moken people and the 2004 Indian Ocean tsunami teaches us about the importance of cultural wisdom and respect for nature. The Moken's knowledge of the sea and its signs helped them survive a deadly disaster. It shows us that listening to the wisdom of elders and learning from nature can save lives.

4.1 What's a hurricane?

A hurricane is a big, powerful storm that forms over warm ocean waters. It has very strong winds and lots of rain. Let's break it down so it's easy to understand:

How Does a Hurricane Start?

- Warm Ocean Water: Hurricanes start over the ocean where the water is really warm. The warm water gives the hurricane its energy.

- Rising Air: The warm water heats the air above it. This warm air rises up into the sky.

- Spinning Storm: As the warm air rises, it starts to spin because of the way the Earth rotates. This spinning air forms a big storm.

Parts of a Hurricane

Eye: The center of the hurricane is called the "eye." The eye is usually calm and clear, with very little wind.

Eye Wall: Around the eye is the "eye wall." This is where the strongest winds and heaviest rain are found. It's the most dangerous part of the hurricane.

Rain Bands: These are long, curved lines of clouds and rain that extend out from the eye wall. They can bring heavy rain and strong winds far from the center of the storm.

What Can Hurricanes Do?

- Strong Winds: Hurricanes have very strong winds that can knock down trees, power lines, and even buildings.

- Heavy Rain: Hurricanes bring a lot of rain, which can cause flooding. Flooding happens when there is too much water and it covers the land.

- Storm Surge: This is a big rise in the ocean level caused by the hurricane's winds pushing water toward the shore. It can cause even more flooding.

How Can We Stay Safe During a Hurricane?

Evacuation Plans: Sometimes, people need to leave their homes and go to a safer place. This is called evacuation. It's important to listen to the news and follow instructions.

Emergency Kits: Having a kit with water, food, flashlights, and other essentials can help you stay safe if you need to stay inside during the storm.

Staying Informed: Watching the news or listening to the radio can help you know what's happening with the hurricane and what you should do.

Remember:

A hurricane is a very big and powerful storm that forms over warm ocean water. It has strong winds, heavy rain, and can cause flooding. By understanding hurricanes and knowing what to do, we can stay safe and be prepared.

4.2 Hurricane Katrina (2005): The Superdome Shelter

The Storm Approaches

In August 2005, a powerful storm called Hurricane Katrina was heading towards New Orleans, a city in Louisiana. The news warned everyone that the hurricane would be very dangerous, with strong winds and heavy rain. People were told to evacuate and find safe places to stay. Many left the city, but some could not, and they needed a safe place to go.

Seeking Shelter in the Superdome

The Superdome, a large stadium in New Orleans, was opened as a shelter for those who could not leave the city. Thousands of people, including families with children, elderly folks, and people with disabilities, went to the Superdome seeking safety from the storm.

Among them was a young boy named Jamal, his little sister Aaliyah, and their mother. They packed a small bag with some clothes, snacks, and water, and headed to the Superdome. Jamal was worried, but he tried to stay brave for his sister.

The Storm Hits

When Hurricane Katrina hit, the winds howled fiercely, and the rain poured down like never before. Inside the Superdome, people could hear the storm raging outside. The power went out, and it became very hot and dark inside. The roof of the Superdome even started leaking in some places.

The conditions were tough, and everyone felt scared and uncomfortable. But amidst the fear and uncertainty, something amazing happened. People started helping each other.

Acts of Kindness

Jamal and his family sat next to an elderly couple who looked very worried. Jamal's mother noticed they didn't have much food, so she shared some of their snacks with them. "Thank you so much," said the elderly woman, smiling kindly at Jamal's mother.

Jamal saw other acts of kindness too. A group of teenagers helped carry water and supplies to those who couldn't move easily. People shared their blankets and offered comforting words to each other. Despite the difficult conditions, everyone tried to make the best of the situation by being kind and supportive.

The Spirit of Community

Jamal found a friend in the Superdome, a boy named Malik, who was about his age. They played simple games and told stories to pass the time. "It's scary, but I'm glad we're here together," said Malik. Jamal agreed, feeling a bit more at ease knowing he wasn't alone.

One night, the storm was particularly loud, and Aaliyah started to cry. Jamal hugged her tightly and whispered, "It's okay, Aaliyah. We're safe here, and Mom is right beside us." His calm words helped his sister feel better, and she soon fell asleep.

The Aftermath

After a few days, the storm passed, but the city was flooded and badly damaged. The people in the Superdome still had to wait for help to arrive. Rescuers eventually came, bringing food, water, and medical supplies. Slowly, the people were moved to safer places where they could start to rebuild their lives.

Jamal and his family were taken to a shelter where they were given food, clothes, and a place to stay. They were grateful to the rescuers and to all the people who had helped each other during the difficult days in the Superdome.

Lessons Learned

The experience of being in the Superdome during Hurricane Katrina taught Jamal many important lessons. He saw how people's kindness and willingness to help each other made a big difference. It showed him the strength of community and how, even in the worst situations, people can come together to support one another.

For young readers, this story highlights the courage and generosity that can shine through during crises. It teaches us that helping others, staying calm, and being kind can make difficult times a little bit easier for everyone. Jamal's experience in the Superdome during Hurricane Katrina is a powerful reminder of the importance of community and the spirit of helping others.

4.3 Hurricane Heart: Family Survival in Puerto Rico

A Storm Approaches

In September 2017, a powerful hurricane named Maria was heading toward Puerto Rico. The weather reports warned that it would be a very strong storm with fierce winds and heavy rain. Many people prepared their homes, gathering supplies and making sure their families were safe.

The Rivera Family

The Rivera family lived in a small town in Puerto Rico. The family included Mama, Papa, 10-year-old Elena, and her little brother, 6-year-old Mateo. They loved their home and the beautiful island, but they were worried about the hurricane. They decided to prepare as best they could.

Preparing for the Storm

Mama and Papa gathered food, water, flashlights, and batteries. They boarded up the windows to protect them from the strong winds. "We need to stay inside and stay safe," said Papa. "Remember, we are together, and we will get through this."

Elena helped by making sure they had plenty of blankets and games to keep Mateo calm and entertained. She also filled containers with water, just in case they needed extra.

The Hurricane Hits

When Hurricane Maria finally hit, the winds howled like a giant monster outside their house. The rain poured down heavily, and the trees bent and swayed under the force of the wind. The Riveras stayed in a small, safe room in the center of their house, away from windows.

Elena held Mateo's hand and whispered, "It's okay, Mateo. We are safe here with Mama and Papa." Mama and Papa hugged them tightly, comforting them as the storm raged on.

Staying Strong Together

The storm lasted all night. The noise was scary, but the Riveras stayed close and supported each other. They played games, told stories, and sang songs to keep their spirits up. Elena was brave and helped Mama take care of Mateo, who was frightened by the loud noises.

The Aftermath

When the storm finally passed, the Riveras came out of their safe room to see the damage. Their house had been damaged by the wind, and the garden was flooded. Many trees had fallen, and the streets were filled with debris. It was a difficult sight to see, but they were grateful to be safe.

Helping the Community

Papa said, "Now it's time to help our neighbors." The Riveras went outside and started cleaning up their yard. They also checked on their neighbors to make sure everyone was okay. The community came together, helping each other clear debris, share food and water, and offer comfort.

Elena and Mateo helped by picking up branches and bringing water to people who needed it. They felt proud to be helping their community.

Rebuilding with Courage

The days after the hurricane were hard, but the Riveras showed great courage and resilience. They worked together to repair their home and help their neighbors. Elena and Mateo learned that even though the storm had been very scary, their family's love and support made them strong.

Papa said, "We will rebuild, and we will be even stronger than before." The Riveras knew that as long as they were together, they could face any challenge.

A Lesson in Courage and Unity

The story of the Rivera family and Hurricane Maria teaches us about the power of courage and unity. Even in the face of a terrible storm, the family stayed strong and helped each other. Their actions show that working together and supporting one another can help us overcome difficult times.

For young readers, this story reminds us that courage isn't just about being brave during the storm but also about helping each other and rebuilding together afterward. The Rivera family's experience during Hurricane Maria is a powerful example of love, resilience, and the strength of a united family.

DESERT DETERMINATION

5.1 What's the Sahara and a sandstorm?

The **Sahara** is the largest **desert** in the world. A desert is a place where it's very dry, and there is very little water. The Sahara is so big that it covers much of **North Africa**. It's a hot and sandy place, but there's much more to know about it!

How Big is the Sahara?

The Sahara Desert is **huge**! It stretches over 3.6 million square miles, which is almost as big as the whole United States! It covers countries like Egypt, Algeria, Libya, and many others in northern Africa. If you were to walk across the Sahara, it would take you many, many days to get from one side to the other.

What's the Weather Like?

In the Sahara, it gets **very hot** during the day. In some places, the temperature can reach over 120°F (50°C)! It's so hot that most animals and people have to find shade during the day. But what's surprising is that the desert can also get **really cold** at night. Sometimes, the temperature drops below freezing!

What Do You See in the Sahara?

When you think of the Sahara, you probably picture lots of **sand**, and that's true! There are **sand dunes**, which are big hills made of sand, that move with the wind. Some of these dunes are as tall as buildings! But the Sahara isn't just sand. There are also **rocky mountains**, **gravel plains**, and even some small **oases**, which are places where water and plants can be found.

Who Lives in the Sahara?

Even though the Sahara is very dry and hot, people have lived there for thousands of years! Some of the people are called **nomads**, which means they move from place to place with their animals like camels and goats. The **Tuareg** people are one of the groups who live in the Sahara. They wear special clothing to protect themselves from the heat and sand.

Animals in the Sahara

You might think that animals can't survive in the Sahara, but there are animals that are specially adapted to live there. For example, **camels** are often called the "ships of the desert" because they can travel long distances without needing much water. There are also **fennec foxes**, with big ears to help keep them cool, and even some **snakes** and **lizards** that live in the sand.

The Importance of the Sahara

The Sahara is important for many reasons. It's a place full of history, with ancient pyramids, ruins, and cave paintings that show us how people lived long ago. The desert also plays a big role in the weather patterns of the world. The winds that blow across the Sahara carry dust that travels all the way to the Amazon rainforest!

What is a Sandstorm in the Sahara?

A sandstorm is when strong winds pick up a lot of sand and dust from the ground and blow it through the air. These storms can happen very quickly, especially in big deserts like the Sahara. Let's learn more about what happens during a sandstorm and why they can be so powerful.

How Do Sandstorms Happen?

o Strong Winds: Sandstorms begin when the wind gets really strong. In the Sahara, the desert is flat and open, so the wind can move very fast. There's nothing to block it, like trees or buildings, so the wind keeps gaining speed.

o Picking Up Sand and Dust: When the wind blows over the sandy ground, it picks up tiny grains of sand and dust. The wind can lift this sand high into the air, creating a thick cloud of sand that can stretch for miles.

o Spreading Across the Desert: The wind can carry the sandstorm across a large area of the desert. Sometimes, these sandstorms can even travel to other countries! The sand and dust get blown far from the desert, and the storm can last for hours.

What Happens During a Sandstorm?

During a sandstorm, the air is filled with sand and dust, making it hard to see or breathe. The sky can turn dark, even if it's the middle of the day. The wind blows very hard, and the sand moves so fast that it feels like it's stinging your skin if you're outside. That's why it's important to take shelter when a sandstorm happens.

People who live in the desert, like the Tuareg, wear special clothing to protect themselves during a sandstorm. They cover their faces with scarves to keep the sand out of their eyes and mouths.

Why Are Sandstorms Dangerous?

- Low Visibility: When there's so much sand in the air, it's hard to see anything, which can make it dangerous for people to travel or drive during a storm.

- Breathing Problems: The sand and dust can make it hard to breathe, especially for people with health problems. That's why it's important to cover your face or stay inside during a sandstorm.

- Strong Winds: The wind in a sandstorm can be very strong, blowing away light objects and damaging buildings or tents.

What Can You Do During a Sandstorm?

✓ Stay Inside: If you see a sandstorm coming, the safest thing to do is go indoors or find shelter. Staying inside helps protect you from the flying sand and strong winds.

✓ Cover Up: If you're outside and can't find shelter right away, cover your mouth and nose with a scarf or piece of cloth to keep the sand out of your lungs. Protect your eyes with goggles or wrap something around your head.

✓ Stay Low: If the wind is too strong, it's a good idea to stay low to the ground, like next to a large rock or wall, to protect yourself from the blowing sand.

5.2 Friends lost in the Sahara

An Exciting Desert Adventure

One summer, a group of friends decided to go on a special adventure—a trek through the vast **Sahara Desert**. There were four friends: **Amir**, who loved exploring, **Leila**, who had read many books about the desert, Sam, who was great with maps, and Nina, who always knew how to stay calm in tough situations.

They were excited to see the towering sand dunes, the endless horizon, and the beautiful, clear skies. They had a guide with them, but on their third day in the desert, something unexpected happened.

The Sandstorm Hits

As the group was walking across the sand, the wind began to pick up. At first, it was just a light breeze, but soon, it became much stronger. Amir looked up and saw a huge cloud of sand swirling in the distance, coming straight toward them.

"It's a sandstorm!" Leila shouted. The sky darkened, and the air filled with sand. They could barely see a few feet in front of them. Their guide tried to lead them to safety, but the storm was so fierce that they got separated.

Lost in the Desert

When the storm finally calmed down, the friends realized they were alone. The desert looked different—like a giant, empty sea of sand. They were scared but knew they had to stay strong and work together if they wanted to survive.

"We need to stay calm," said Nina. "We can get through this if we help each other."

Amir checked their supplies. "We don't have much water left," he said. "We'll need to save what we have and only drink small sips."

Rationing Water and Finding a Way

The friends decided to **ration** their water, each taking tiny sips to make it last as long as possible. They also shared the little food they had, making sure everyone had enough energy to keep going.

Sam had a map, but without landmarks, it was hard to tell where they were. Then, Leila had an idea. "We can use the **stars** to guide us!" she said. She remembered from her books that people in the desert had used the stars to find their way for thousands of years.

At night, when the sky was clear, Sam and Leila used the stars to figure out which direction they should go. "If we keep heading north, we might find help," Sam said.

A Test of Courage

The days were hot, and the nights were cold, but the friends stuck together. They kept walking, encouraging each other when they felt tired or scared. "We can do this," Amir said. "We just need to stay focused."

During the day, they would cover themselves with their scarves to protect their faces from the sun and wind. At night, they would huddle together to stay warm. Even though they were lost, they never gave up.

Finding Help

On the fourth day, after walking for hours, they saw something in the distance—a small group of tents. It was a nomadic tribe that lived in the desert, moving from place to place. The friends felt a wave of relief. They had found help!

The people from the tribe welcomed the friends warmly. They gave them food, water, and a place to rest. "You are brave to have survived the storm and found your way here," one of the tribe's leaders said.

The friends stayed with the tribe for a short time, and then the nomads helped them find their way back to a nearby village. Soon, they were reunited with their guide and their families, who were so happy and proud of their courage.

A Lesson in Courage and Teamwork

The friends learned a lot from their time in the Sahara. They learned that even in the scariest situations, staying calm and helping each other can make all the difference. By using their knowledge and working as a team, they survived the harsh desert and found their way to safety.

For young readers, this story shows that **courage** isn't just about being strong—it's about staying calm, using what you know, and never giving up, even when things seem impossible. The friends' adventure in the Sahara reminds us that, together, we can overcome any challenge.

6.1 What's a flood?

A flood happens when there is too much water in an area, and it covers the ground that is usually dry. Let's find out more about how floods happen and what they can do.

How Do Floods Happen?

1. **Heavy Rain:** Sometimes, it rains a lot in a short period. When the ground can't absorb all the water, the extra water starts to build up and can cause a flood.

2. **Overflowing Rivers and Lakes:** When it rains too much, rivers and lakes can fill up with water. If they get too full, the water can spill over the sides and flood the surrounding areas.

3. **Melting Snow:** In places where it snows, warm weather can melt the snow very quickly. The melting snow turns into water, which can flow into rivers and lakes, making them overflow and cause floods.

4. **Broken Dams:** Dams are structures that hold back water in rivers or lakes. If a dam breaks, a lot of water can rush out all at once, causing a flood.

What Happens During a Flood?

- Covering the Ground: When a flood happens, water covers the streets, fields, and even houses. The water can be very deep, making it hard for people to walk or drive.

- Strong Currents: Floodwater can move very quickly, like a river. The strong currents can carry away cars, trees, and even buildings.

- Damage: Floods can damage homes, roads, and other buildings. The water can ruin furniture, appliances, and other belongings inside houses

How Can We Stay Safe During a Flood?

o Stay Away from Floodwater: Floodwater can be dangerous. It can be very deep, move quickly, and contain things like sharp objects or harmful chemicals. It's important to stay away from it.

o Go to Higher Ground: If there is a flood warning, it's important to move to higher ground where the water can't reach. This could be a hill, a tall building, or any place that is above the water level.

o Listen to Authorities: Pay attention to news and weather reports. Follow the advice of local authorities, like firefighters or police, who can tell you what to do to stay safe.

What Can We Learn from Floods?

Floods can be very scary, but they also teach us important lessons. They remind us to be prepared and to know what to do in an emergency. It's important to have a plan and to know where to go if a flood happens. We also learn the importance of helping each other and staying calm.

Remember:

A flood happens when there is too much water in an area, and it covers the ground. Floods can be caused by heavy rain, overflowing rivers or lakes, melting snow, or broken dams. They can cause a lot of damage, but by staying safe, going to higher ground, and listening to authorities, we can protect ourselves. Being prepared and knowing what to do can make a big difference during a flood.

6.2 A Tale of Courage

A Rainy Season Begins

In late 2010, Queensland, Australia, began to experience heavy rains. It was the rainy season, but this year, the rain seemed to never stop. Rivers overflowed, and soon, towns and cities were filled with water. People were starting to worry.

A Small Town in Danger

In a small town, there lived a family named the Taylors. The Taylors included Mom, Dad, 12-year-old Jack, and his little sister, 8-year-old Lily. They loved their home but were concerned about the rising waters. One night, the rain was so heavy that it caused the river near their house to flood.

Preparing to Leave

Mom and Dad decided it was time to leave their home to stay safe. "We need to go to higher ground," Dad said. "It's not safe here with all this water." They quickly packed their important belongings and prepared to leave.

Jack helped by gathering their favorite books and toys, and Lily made sure they had snacks for the journey. They were sad to leave their home but knew it was the right thing to do.

The Flood Comes

As they were getting ready to leave, the water started to come into their yard and then into their house. The Taylors hurried out to their car, which was parked on the street, but the water was rising fast. They knew they couldn't drive through the floodwaters.

A Heroic Rescue

Just when they didn't know what to do, a neighbor named Mr. Johnson came by in a small boat. "Hop in!" he shouted. "I'll take you to safety!" The Taylors climbed into the boat, and Mr. Johnson paddled them to higher ground, away from the dangerous water.

Jack and Lily were scared but also felt safe knowing they were with their family and Mr. Johnson. They watched as the floodwaters covered their neighborhood, but they were thankful to be safe.

Staying Strong Together

On higher ground, the Taylors found a community center where other families were taking shelter. They were given warm blankets and food, and they met other children who were also there because of the flood.

Jack and Lily made new friends and played games to pass the time. They learned that many people had to leave their homes, just like them. Everyone was helping each other, sharing food, and comforting those who were scared.

The Floodwaters Recede

After several days, the rain finally stopped, and the floodwaters began to go down. The Taylors returned to their home to see the damage. It was hard to see their house filled with mud and water, but they were determined to clean up and rebuild.

A Community Rebuilds

The whole community came together to help each other. People shared tools and supplies, and everyone worked hard to repair the damage caused by the flood. The Taylors were grateful for the help and support from their neighbors.

A Lesson in Courage

The Queensland floods taught Jack, Lily, and their family important lessons about courage and community. They learned that even in the face of a disaster, people could unite to help each other and improve things.

For young readers, this story shows that courage means not only being brave in difficult times but also helping others and working together. The Taylors' experience during the Queensland floods is a reminder that with courage and unity, we can overcome any challenge.

7.1 Amazon forests

The Amazon is one of the largest and most famous rainforests in the world. It's a special place full of trees, animals, and plants. Let's find out more about why the Amazon is so amazing!

Where Are the Amazon Forests?

The Amazon rainforest is located in South America. It covers parts of several countries, but most of it is in Brazil. The Amazon is so big that it's sometimes called the "lungs of the Earth" because it produces a lot of the oxygen we breathe.

What Is a Rainforest?

A rainforest is a type of forest that gets a lot of rain, almost every day. This makes it a very wet and warm place, which is perfect for many different kinds of plants and animals.

What Can You Find in the Amazon Forests?

- **Trees and Plants**: The Amazon is filled with thousands of different types of trees and plants. Some trees are so tall they reach the sky! There are also many colorful flowers and interesting plants that can only be found there.

- **Animals**: The Amazon is home to a huge variety of animals. You can find monkeys, parrots, jaguars, and even pink dolphins in its rivers. There are also many insects, frogs, and other creatures living in the forest.

- **Rivers**: The Amazon River, one of the longest rivers in the world, flows through the rainforest. It's a big part of the Amazon's ecosystem, providing water and a home for many animals.

Why Are the Amazon Forests Important?

- **Biodiversity**: The Amazon has one of the highest levels of biodiversity in the world, which means it has many different kinds of living things. This diversity is important for the health of our planet.

- **Climate**: The trees in the Amazon help control the Earth's climate by absorbing carbon dioxide and producing oxygen. This helps keep our air clean and our planet cool.

- **Medicine**: Many of the plants in the Amazon are used to make medicines. Scientists study these plants to find new ways to treat illnesses.

Protecting the Amazon

The Amazon rainforest is very important, but it's also at risk from things like deforestation (cutting down trees) and climate change. It's important for everyone to help protect the rainforest so it can continue to be a home for many plants and animals and help keep our planet healthy.

Remember:

The Amazon Forests are a huge and beautiful rainforest in South America. They are full of amazing plants, animals, and rivers. The Amazon helps produce oxygen, supports biodiversity, and provides resources for medicine. It's a very special place that we need to protect for the future.

7.2 Wonderful Rescue in the Amazon Forests: A Story of Courage

An Exciting Adventure

In the summer of 2020, a group of friends went on an exciting adventure to the Amazon rainforest. The group included Anna, who loved animals and plants; Ben, who was always curious about nature; Carla, who enjoyed taking photos of everything she saw; and Diego, a local guide who knew the forest very well.

The Amazon rainforest is a huge and beautiful place with tall trees, colorful birds, and many amazing creatures. The friends were excited to explore and learn about the different plants and animals that lived there.

The Unexpected Flood

One day, while they were deep in the forest, the sky suddenly turned dark. Thick clouds gathered, and soon it began to rain heavily. The rain didn't stop, and the rivers started to rise quickly. The friends realized they were in danger of being caught in a flood.

Diego, the guide, knew they needed to find higher ground to stay safe. "We have to move quickly and find a safe place before the water gets too high," he said. The friends followed him, but the water was rising fast, and it became harder to walk through the forest.

Finding Shelter

Diego led them to a large tree with thick branches. "We can climb up this tree to stay above the water," he said. The friends climbed the tree and found a sturdy branch to sit on. From there, they could see the water rising below them, covering the ground where they had just been walking.

Even though they were safe for now, they knew they needed to find a better solution. Anna noticed some large logs floating by and got an idea. "What if we build a raft?" she suggested. "We can use the logs to make a raft and float to safety."

Building the Raft

Ben and Diego thought it was a great idea. They carefully climbed down the tree and started gathering the large logs. Carla used some strong vines she had found to tie the logs together. It was hard work, but they didn't give up. They worked as a team, and soon they had built a sturdy raft.

The friends climbed onto the raft, and Diego used a long stick to push them through the water. The current was strong, but Diego was very skilled at guiding the raft. They floated through the flooded forest, looking for a safe place to land.

The Rescue

After a few hours, they heard the sound of a helicopter. It was a rescue team searching for people who were stranded by the flood. The friends waved their arms and shouted to get the helicopter's attention. The helicopter saw them and hovered above.

A rescuer was lowered down and helped each of them onto the helicopter. They were airlifted to safety, where they were given food, water, and dry clothes. The friends were relieved and grateful to be rescued.

Lessons Learned

The experience taught the friends many important lessons about courage and teamwork. Anna's idea to build a raft and Diego's knowledge of the forest helped save them. Ben and Carla's hard work and positive attitude kept everyone hopeful. They realized that by working together and staying calm, they could overcome even the most frightening situations.

A Story of Courage

The wonderful rescue in the Amazon forests showed the friends the importance of being brave and thinking quickly. It also taught them that helping each other and staying positive can make a big difference. Their adventure in the Amazon is a story of courage and teamwork that they will always remember.

It reminds us that even in scary situations, we can find solutions and help each other stay safe. The friends' experience in the Amazon rainforest is a powerful example of the strength and bravery that come from sticking together and staying calm.

8.1 What's a wildfire?

A wildfire is a big fire that spreads quickly over a large area, usually in forests, grasslands, or other places with lots of plants. Wildfires can be very dangerous, but they are also a natural part of some ecosystems. Let's find out more about them!

How Do Wildfires Start?

1. **Natural Causes**: Sometimes, wildfires start because of natural events, like lightning strikes. When lightning hits a dry tree or grass, it can start a fire.

2. **Human Activities**: Wildfires can also start because of things people do, like leaving a campfire unattended, burning trash, or accidentally dropping a lit cigarette.

What Makes Wildfires Spread?

- **Dry Conditions**: Wildfires spread more easily when the weather is hot and dry, and there hasn't been much rain. Dry plants and trees catch fire more easily.

- **Wind**: Wind can blow sparks and embers from a wildfire to new areas, starting more fires and making the wildfire spread faster.

- **Fuel**: In a wildfire, "fuel" means anything that can burn, like trees, grass, leaves, and even houses. The more fuel there is, the bigger the fire can get.

The Effects of Wildfires

- **Damage to Nature**: Wildfires can burn down forests and grasslands, destroying the habitats of animals and plants. Some animals can escape, but others may be harmed.

- **Harm to People**: Wildfires can also be dangerous for

people, destroying homes and property. The smoke from wildfires can make it hard to breathe and is especially dangerous for people with health problems.

- **Benefits to Nature**: While wildfires can be harmful, they can also be beneficial in some ways. For example, fires can clear out dead trees and plants, making room for new growth. Some plants even need fire to release their seeds.

How Can We Stay Safe?

- **Fire Safety**: It's important to be careful with fire, especially in places where wildfires can happen. Always put out campfires completely, don't throw lit cigarettes on the ground, and follow local fire safety rules.

- **Evacuation Plans**: In areas prone to wildfires, families should have an evacuation plan. This means knowing the safest routes to leave and having a plan for where to go.

- **Listening to Authorities**: If there is a wildfire, it's important to listen to firefighters and other authorities. They can give advice on when to leave and how to stay safe.

Remember: Wildfires are large, fast-spreading fires that can happen in forests, grasslands, and other areas with lots of plants. They can start naturally or because of human activities. While wildfires can be dangerous and destructive, they can also play a role in nature by helping to renew the land. It's important to be careful with fire and follow safety guidelines to prevent wildfires and stay safe.

8.2. The Great Chicago Fire (1871): The Rush to the Lake

A Busy Night in Chicago

On the evening of October 8, 1871, the city of Chicago was busy and bustling. People were going about their daily routines, children were playing, and families were enjoying their time together. Chicago was a growing city with many wooden buildings, which made it a beautiful but also a very flammable place.

The Fire Begins

Suddenly, a fire broke out in a small barn on the southwest side of the city. The exact cause of the fire is still a mystery, but some say it might have started when a cow knocked over a lantern. Whatever the cause, the fire quickly grew out of control. The flames spread rapidly, jumping from building to building, fueled by the wooden structures and strong winds.

The Flames Spread

As the fire raged through the city, people began to realize the danger they were in. The flames were fierce and unstoppable, consuming everything in their path. The sky turned red with the glow of the fire, and thick smoke filled the air, making it hard to breathe and see.

Fleeing to Safety

During the chaos, families knew they had to act quickly to escape the fire. One brave family, the Johnsons, decided to head towards the shores of Lake Michigan, hoping to find safety in the water. Mr. Johnson, his wife, and their two children, Emma and Jack, hurriedly packed a few essential items and left their home.

"Stay close and hold hands," Mr. Johnson told Emma and Jack. "We need to move fast and stay together."

As they made their way through the crowded streets, they saw many other families doing the same. People were running, carrying their belongings and helping each other. The heat from the fire was intense, and the roar of the flames was deafening.

Reaching the Lake

Finally, after what seemed like an endless journey, the Johnson family reached the shores of Lake Michigan. The cool, blue water offered a stark contrast to the fiery inferno behind them. Many others had also gathered at the lake, seeking refuge from the flames.

The Johnsons, along with other families, waded into the shallow waters of the lake to stay safe from the heat and smoke. They stayed there, holding onto each other and offering comfort, while they watched their city burn.

Lessons in Courage and Quick Thinking

The Great Chicago Fire burned for two days, destroying much of the city. When it was finally over, the people of Chicago faced the daunting task of rebuilding their lives and their city. Despite the devastation, the courage and quick thinking of the residents helped save many lives.

The Johnson family, like many others, showed bravery and resourcefulness by evacuating quickly and finding safety. Their story teaches us important lessons about fire safety and the need to act swiftly in an emergency. Knowing where to go and what to do can make a big difference.

Rebuilding Together

After the fire, the people of Chicago came together to rebuild their city. They worked hard to create stronger buildings and better fire safety measures to prevent.

9.1 What's a Volcano?

A volcano is like a big mountain, but it can sometimes erupt with lots of hot, melted rock called lava, along with ash and gases. Let's find out more about how volcanoes work!

How Do Volcanoes Form?

1. **Inside the Earth**: Deep inside the Earth, it's very hot. There's a layer of hot, melted rock called magma.
2. **Magma Rises**: Sometimes, the magma finds a way to move up through cracks in the Earth's crust (the outer layer of the Earth). When this happens, it can form a volcano.
3. **Eruption**: When there's too much pressure inside the volcano, it can erupt. During an eruption, magma comes out of the volcano. When magma reaches the surface, it's called lava.

Parts of a Volcano

- **Crater**: This is the bowl-shaped area at the top of the volcano where the lava comes out during an eruption.
- **Vent**: The vent is like a pathway through which the magma travels to the surface.
- **Lava Flow**: This is the stream of lava that flows down the sides of the volcano during an eruption.
- **Ash Cloud**: Sometimes, volcanoes also send out a big cloud of ash, which is tiny bits of rock and minerals.

What Happens During an Eruption?

- **Lava Flows**: Lava can flow down the sides of the volcano. It's very hot and can destroy everything in its path.
- **Ash and Gas**: The eruption can also release ash and gases into the air. The ash can fall back down to the ground and cover buildings, plants, and other things.
- **Earthquakes**: Sometimes, small earthquakes can happen before or during a volcanic eruption.

Why Are Volcanoes Important?

- **New Land**: When the lava cools down, it becomes solid rock. Over time, this can create new land.
- **Rich Soil**: The ash and lava can break down and turn into very rich soil, which is great for growing plants.
- **Beautiful Landscapes**: Volcanoes create interesting and beautiful landscapes, like mountains and islands.

Staying Safe Near Volcanoes

If you live near a volcano, it's important to listen to scientists and local authorities. They can tell you if the volcano might erupt and what to do to stay safe.

Remember:

A volcano is a mountain that can erupt with lava, ash, and gases. It's formed by magma coming up from deep inside the Earth. While volcanoes can be dangerous when they erupt, they also create beautiful landscapes and rich soil.

9.2 The 1980 Mount St. Helens Eruption: Harry R. Truman's Legacy

A Quiet Life by the Mountain

Harry R. Truman was a man who loved his home by the beautiful Mount St. Helens in Washington State. He owned a lodge called Spirit Lake Lodge, where he welcomed visitors who came to enjoy the scenic views of the mountain and the peaceful lake. Harry was known for his friendly personality and his deep connection to the land.

The Warning Signs

In early 1980, scientists noticed something unusual about Mount St. Helens. The ground was shaking more than usual, and there were signs that the volcano might erupt. They warned everyone living near the mountain to evacuate for their safety.

Many people packed their belongings and left, but Harry decided to stay. He had lived by the mountain for over 50 years and didn't want to leave his home and his beloved lodge. "This is my home," he said. "I'm not going anywhere."

The Eruption Begins

On May 18, 1980, Mount St. Helens erupted with incredible force. The eruption sent ash and rocks high into the sky and caused a massive landslide. The once beautiful landscape was dramatically reshaped. The blast was so powerful that it flattened trees, filled the air with ash, and sent hot gas and lava flowing down the mountainside.

Harry's Courage and Legacy

Despite the danger, Harry stayed at Spirit Lake Lodge. His decision to stay made him a symbol of resistance and attachment to home. He loved his home so much that he chose to face the eruption rather than leave.

Harry's story is one of great courage, but it also teaches an important lesson. While Harry's bravery is admired, it is also a reminder of the power of nature and the importance of listening to safety warnings. The scientists' warnings were given to protect lives, and it's important to heed such advice in dangerous situations.

Remembering Mount St. Helens

The eruption of Mount St. Helens changed the landscape forever. It created a huge crater at the top of the mountain and left the surrounding area covered in ash and debris. It also taught us valuable lessons about the power of nature and the importance of safety.

Harry R. Truman's legacy lives on as a reminder of the deep connection people can have to their homes. His story encourages us to be brave but also to be wise. When experts warn us about danger, it's important to listen and take action to stay safe.

A Lesson in Courage and Wisdom

For young readers, the story of Harry R. Truman and the eruption of Mount St. Helens is a lesson in both courage and the importance of listening to safety advice. It shows that while it's important to be brave and care deeply about our homes, it's also crucial to respect the power of nature and follow expert warnings to protect ourselves and our loved ones.

Harry's story will always be remembered as a symbol of courage and a reminder of the incredible force of nature. By learning from his experience, we can understand the importance of being both brave and wise in the face of natural disasters.

SNOWSTORM STRUGGLE

10.1 What's a Snowstorm?

A snowstorm is a type of winter storm that brings lots of snow, strong winds, and cold temperatures. Let's find out more about what happens during a snowstorm and how we can stay safe!

What Happens in a Snowstorm?

1. **Lots of Snow**: During a snowstorm, a lot of snow falls from the sky. The snow can cover the ground, roads, and everything outside, making it look like a winter wonderland.
2. **Strong Winds**: Snowstorms often come with strong winds. These winds can blow the snow around, making it hard to see. This is called a "blizzard" when the wind and snow are very strong.
3. **Cold Temperatures**: Snowstorms bring very cold weather. It's important to wear warm clothes like coats, hats, and gloves to stay warm if you go outside.

How Do Snowstorms Form?

Snowstorms form when cold air mixes with warm, moist air. The warm air rises and cools down, turning the moisture into snowflakes. If the conditions are right, the snowflakes fall to the ground, creating a snowstorm.

Effects of Snowstorms
- **Snow Cover**: Snowstorms can leave a thick layer of snow on the ground. This can make it hard for cars to drive and people to walk.

- **Power Outages**: The heavy snow and strong winds can sometimes knock down power lines, causing power outages. This means there could be no electricity for a while.
- **School and Business Closures**: Sometimes, snowstorms are so strong that schools and businesses close to keep people safe. This is often called a "snow day."

How Can We Stay Safe in a Snowstorm?

- **Stay Indoors**: The best place to be during a snowstorm is inside your home, where it's warm and safe.
- **Bundle Up**: If you need to go outside, wear lots of warm layers, including a hat, gloves, and a scarf. This helps protect you from the cold.
- **Have Supplies**: It's a good idea to have extra food, water, and blankets at home in case the storm is very strong and you can't go out.
- **Be Careful on the Roads**: If you have to travel, make sure to drive slowly and carefully, as roads can be slippery.

Remember:

A snowstorm is a winter storm that brings lots of snow, strong winds, and cold temperatures. They can be fun to watch and play in, but it's important to stay safe and warm. By being prepared and careful, we can enjoy the beauty of a snowstorm while staying safe.

10.2 A Story of Courage

The Adventurous Trip

In the summer of 2018, a group of friends went on a hiking trip in the beautiful Swiss Alps. Among them were Luca, a young mountaineer who loved climbing; Jonas, Luca's best friend who enjoyed exploring nature; Emma, a girl who loved taking pictures of the mountains; and Max, who was excited to see the snow even in summer.

The Alps were magnificent, with towering peaks, green meadows, and clear blue skies. The friends were excited to hike up the mountain trails, enjoy the fresh air, and take in the stunning views.

The Unexpected Storm

One afternoon, as they were hiking higher up the mountain, dark clouds suddenly appeared. The wind began to blow harder, and the temperature dropped quickly. Before they knew it, a severe snowstorm hit the area. Snow and ice started falling heavily, and the visibility became very poor. The friends were caught in the middle of the storm, far from their base camp.

Luca, who had experience with mountain climbing, knew they needed to find shelter quickly. "We have to stay together and find a safe place," he shouted over the howling wind.

Finding Shelter

Luca remembered a small mountain hut not too far from where they were. He led the group through the blinding snow, carefully guiding them along the trail. The snow was deep, and the wind was strong, but they trusted Luca and followed him closely.

After a challenging trek, they finally reached the mountain hut. It was a small, sturdy wooden cabin built for hikers to use in emergencies. The hut provided shelter from the storm, and the friends quickly went inside, relieved to be out of the freezing wind and snow.

Staying Calm and Working Together

The friends knew they had to stay calm inside the hut and work together to get through the storm. They had limited supplies but enough to keep warm and safe. Luca started a small fire in the hut's fireplace to provide heat. Emma used her first aid kit to treat Max's frostbite, and Jonas found blankets and distributed them among the group.

They sat close to the fire, sharing stories and singing songs to keep their spirits up. Luca reminded them that staying positive and hopeful was important. "The storm will pass, and we'll be rescued soon," he said confidently.

The Rescue

The storm raged on for two days, but the friends stayed safe and warm inside the hut. On the third day, they heard the sound of a helicopter. Rescuers were searching for hikers who had been caught in the storm. The friends quickly went outside and waved their bright-colored jackets to signal the helicopter.

The rescuers spotted them and soon landed near the hut. The friends were airlifted to safety, and they were very grateful for the brave rescuers who had come to help them. They were also thankful for Luca's courage and knowledge, which had kept them safe during the storm.

A Lesson in Courage and Teamwork

The mountain rescue in the Alps taught the friends valuable lessons about courage and teamwork. Luca's experience and calm leadership helped them find shelter and stay safe. Working together and supporting each other made a scary situation much more manageable.

This story shows young readers that being brave and helping each other is very important, especially in difficult times. It also reminds us that knowledge and preparation can make a big difference in emergencies. The Friends' adventure in the Alps is a story of courage, friendship, and the strength of working together.

11.1 What's an Avalanche?

An avalanche is when a large amount of snow suddenly slides down the side of a mountain. Avalanches can be very fast and powerful, and they can happen in snowy, mountainous areas. Let's explore how avalanches happen and why they can be so dangerous.

How Do Avalanches Happen?

- **Heavy Snowfall**: Avalanches often start after a lot of snow has fallen. When too much snow piles up on a mountain, it can become unstable, which means it can't stay in place.
- **Weak Layers of Snow**: Snow on a mountain settles in layers. Sometimes, the layers of snow underneath are weaker than the layers on top. This can make the snow on top slide off easily, just like when a stack of papers might fall if there's something slippery underneath.
- **Triggers**: Sometimes, an avalanche can be triggered by something that disturbs the snow. It could be loud sounds, such as a snowmobile or a person skiing, or even strong winds. These movements shake the snow, causing it to slide.

What Happens During an Avalanche?

When an avalanche begins, tons of snow rush down the mountain, picking up speed as it moves. It can carry snow, rocks, trees, and anything in its path. Avalanches move very fast, sometimes faster than a car, which makes it hard to escape if you are in the way.

The snow can bury anything underneath it, making it

difficult for people or animals to breathe if they get caught in an avalanche.

Staying Safe in Avalanche Areas

- **Stay Alert**: If you're skiing or hiking in a snowy area, it's important to listen to weather reports and look for signs of avalanches. If the area looks unstable or if there's been a lot of fresh snow, it's better to stay away from steep slopes.
- **Avalanche Gear**: People who go into areas where avalanches are common sometimes carry special gear like beacons, which help rescuers find them in case they get trapped.
- **Avoid Loud Noises or Disturbing the Snow**: In areas where avalanches are likely, it's important to move carefully and avoid making loud noises or sudden movements that could trigger a snow slide.

Why Are Avalanches Dangerous?

Avalanches are dangerous because they happen very quickly and can bury people or buildings under deep snow. They can destroy trees, houses, and roads in their path. That's why it's important to be very careful when you are in places where avalanches might happen.

What Can We Learn?

Avalanches show us how powerful nature can be, especially in the mountains. And just like in the stories of brave skiers and mountain climbers, we can learn that staying calm and making good choices can help keep us safe.

11.2 Skiing in the Rockies

A Fun Day in the Mountains

One winter day, a group of friends decided to go skiing in the beautiful Rocky Mountains. The group included Sarah, who was an experienced skier, and her friends, Mia, Ben, and Jake.

They were excited to spend the day on the snowy slopes, racing down the mountain and enjoying the fresh, crisp air.

The mountains were covered in thick, white snow, and the sun was shining brightly. It seemed like the perfect day for adventure. But deep in the mountains, things can change quickly, and the group was about to face a scary situation they didn't expect.

The Avalanche Begins

As the friends were skiing down a steep slope, they heard a deep, rumbling sound. At first, they didn't know what it was, but then they saw it—an avalanche! A huge wall of snow was rushing down the mountain toward them. It was moving fast and looked dangerous.

"Quick! We have to move!" Sarah shouted. She knew exactly what to do because she had been trained for situations like this. Her friends trusted her and followed her lead without hesitation.

Finding a Safe Spot

Sarah quickly scanned the area and saw a large group of trees not far away. "Head to the trees!" she yelled, knowing that the thick trees would provide some protection from the rushing snow. They skied as fast as they could, trying to reach the safety of the trees before the avalanche caught up with them.

Once they reached the trees, Sarah told everyone to stay close together and crouch down. They huddled near the base of a large tree, holding onto each other as the avalanche roared past them. It was loud and terrifying, but the group stayed calm, trusting Sarah's leadership.

Staying Calm and Calling for Help

After the avalanche passed, everything became quiet again. Snow covered much of the mountain, and it looked very different from just a few minutes ago. The group was safe, but they were stranded on the mountain with no easy way down.

Sarah knew they needed help. She pulled out her phone and called for a rescue team. "We're okay, but we're stuck in the trees after an avalanche," she told the rescuers. The rescuers told her to stay calm and that they would send a team to get them. While they waited, Sarah encouraged her friends to stay positive. "We did the right thing by getting to the trees," she said. "Help is on the way, and we'll be safe soon."

The Rescue

After a short time, the rescue team arrived on snowmobiles. They had special equipment to help people stranded in the snow. The rescuers praised Sarah for her quick thinking and calm leadership. They said that getting to the trees was the best choice, and calling for help right away was exactly what they needed to do.

One by one, the rescuers helped the group down the mountain and brought them to safety. The friends were relieved and grateful to be okay, and they knew that Sarah's courage had saved them from danger.

A Lesson in Courage and Leadership

The avalanche in the Rockies taught the group an important lesson about courage and leadership. Sarah's quick thinking and experience helped keep everyone safe, and her friends trusted her because they knew she was calm and smart in emergencies.

For young readers, this story shows that being brave means staying calm in tough situations and helping others. Sarah's actions remind us that leadership is about making smart decisions and taking care of the people around us.

12.1 What's a typhoon?

A typhoon is a really big and powerful storm that forms over warm ocean waters. It has very strong winds, heavy rain, and can cause big waves in the ocean. Typhoons are similar to hurricanes, but they usually happen in parts of Asia, like Japan, China, and the Philippines.

Let's explore how typhoons form, what happens during a typhoon, and why they can be dangerous.

How Do Typhoons Form?

o **Warm Ocean Water**: Typhoons start over warm parts of the ocean. The warm water heats up the air above it, making the air rise.

o **Rising Air**: As the warm air rises, it creates a big area of low pressure. This makes more air from the surrounding areas move in to fill the space, which then heats up and rises, too.

o **Spinning Wind**: Because the Earth spins, the wind starts to swirl around the center of the storm. This creates a spinning motion, and the typhoon grows bigger and stronger.

o **The Eye**: In the middle of a typhoon is something called "the eye." The eye of the storm is a calm spot where there is no wind or rain. But around the eye, the winds are very strong and dangerous.

What Happens During a Typhoon?

• **Strong Winds**: The winds in a typhoon can be

incredibly strong, often blowing at speeds faster than a car. These winds can knock down trees, buildings, and power lines.

- **Heavy Rain**: Typhoons bring a lot of rain. Sometimes, it can rain so much that streets, houses, and fields get flooded. Floods can be dangerous because the water can rise very quickly.
- **Big Waves**: Typhoons also cause big waves in the ocean, called storm surges. These huge waves can crash onto the shore and cause flooding in coastal areas.

Where Do Typhoons Happen?

Typhoons mostly happen in the western Pacific Ocean, near countries like Japan, the Philippines, China, and Taiwan. The same kind of storm is called a **hurricane** when it happens in the Atlantic Ocean near the United States and the Caribbean.

How Can We Stay Safe During a Typhoon?

1. **Stay Indoors**: During a typhoon, the safest place to be is inside a strong building. It protects you from the winds and the heavy rain.
2. **Prepare**: Before a typhoon hits, it's important to get ready by having enough food, water, and emergency supplies. People also board up their windows to protect them from strong winds.
3. **Listen to Warnings**: Weather experts track typhoons and give warnings when one is coming. It's important to listen to these warnings and follow the instructions from local authorities, like evacuating if needed.

Why Are Typhoons Dangerous?

Typhoons are dangerous because their strong winds and heavy rain can destroy buildings, flood streets, and even cause landslides. The big waves they create can flood coastal areas, putting people and homes at risk. But by being prepared and knowing what to do, we can stay safe during a typhoon.

What Can We Learn?

Typhoons are powerful storms, but if we stay calm and follow safety rules, we can protect ourselves. It's important to listen to weather warnings, stay indoors, and be prepared. Learning about typhoons helps us understand how strong nature can be and what we can do to stay safe when a big storm hits.

12.2 Unity in the Philippines

A Normal Day in the Philippines

It was a bright and sunny day in November 2013 when sisters Maria, who was 12, and her younger sister Sofia, who was 8, were playing outside their home in the Philippines. They lived in a small, peaceful village where they spent most of their time with their family. But on this day, everything was about to change.

News had come that a powerful storm, called Typhoon

Haiyan was heading toward the Philippines. Maria and Sofia's parents told them they needed to get ready because the storm would be very strong. Everyone in the village was preparing, gathering food, and water, and securing their homes.

The Storm Arrives

Soon, the winds started picking up, and the sky turned dark. The rain came down in heavy sheets, and the wind began to howl louder and louder. The family was huddled together inside their home, but as the storm grew stronger, the wind began to tear at the walls of their house.

Suddenly, a giant wave of water, caused by the typhoon, rushed into their village. Maria and Sofia were separated from their parents in the chaos. The water was rising fast, and Maria knew they had to find somewhere safe. "Come on, Sofia! We need to go!" Maria shouted, holding her sister's hand tightly.

Finding Safety in a Tree

With the water rushing around them, Maria spotted a tall, sturdy tree not far away. "Let's climb that tree!" Maria said, and together, the sisters made their way through the water and grabbed onto the tree's branches. They climbed as high as they could, away from the flooding waters below.

The wind was still howling, and the rain kept pouring down, but the tree held firm. Maria and Sofia clung to the branches, scared but knowing that they had each other. "We're going to be okay," Maria reassured her little sister. "Just stay close to me."

Surviving Together

The storm lasted for hours, and Maria and Sofia stayed in the tree, holding on tightly. They were cold and wet, but they didn't give up. To survive, they drank the rainwater and ate some fruits that had fallen from the tree. They worked together to keep each other safe, never letting go of hope.

Maria's courage helped Sofia stay calm, even though they were scared. "We just have to stay strong," Maria said. "Mom and Dad will find us soon."

The Rescue

After what felt like forever, the storm finally passed. The village was badly damaged, and there was water everywhere, but Maria and Sofia were safe in the tree. Soon, rescue teams arrived to help people who had been caught in the storm.

Maria and Sofia were found by a rescue boat, and they were taken to a shelter where they were reunited with their parents. Their family was overjoyed to be together again, and Maria and Sofia's story of sticking together through the storm inspired everyone in their village.

A Lesson in Courage and Unity

Maria and Sofia showed incredible courage during Typhoon Haiyan. Even though they were scared and separated from their family, they stayed strong and supported each other.

Their bravery and unity helped them survive one of the strongest storms ever to hit the Philippines.

12.3 Survival in Taiwan

A Storm Approaches

In August 2009, a powerful storm called **Typhoon Morakot** was heading toward Taiwan. Mei, a 10-year-old girl, and her best friend Jia, who was also 10, lived in a small village in the countryside. The two friends spent every day playing together, exploring their village, and sharing stories. But when Typhoon Morakot came, their lives changed in a way they never expected.

The people in the village were warned about the storm, and everyone tried to prepare. Mei and Jia's families gathered food, water, and other supplies, hoping they would stay safe during the storm. But Typhoon Morakot was much stronger than anyone thought.

The Flood Begins

When the typhoon hit, it brought heavy rain and strong winds. The rain didn't stop for days, and soon the rivers overflowed, flooding the streets and homes in the village. Mei and Jia were at home when the water started to rise very quickly. Their families were separated by the rushing water, and the two girls found themselves alone, trapped in their flooded village.

Mei looked at Jia and said, "We have to stay together, Jia. Let's find somewhere safe." They spotted a tall house with a flat roof nearby. Even though the water was rising fast, the girls worked together to make their way through the deep water. Holding onto each other, they climbed onto the roof of the house, away from the flood.

Sticking Together on the Rooftop

Once they reached the rooftop, Mei and Jia huddled together. The rain was still pouring, and the wind was strong, but they felt safer being above the water. They had brought a small bag of food and water with them, but it wasn't much. Mei knew they had to make it last.

"We'll share everything we have," Mei said. The girls carefully ate small portions of the food and drank only a little water at a time. They encouraged each other to stay strong, even though they were scared and didn't know how long they would have to wait for help.

At night, they tried to stay warm by wrapping themselves in a blanket they had found. Jia was frightened by the loud wind and rain, but Mei comforted her, saying, "We're going to be okay. As long as we stay together, we'll be safe."

Waiting for Help

Days passed, and the rain finally began to slow down. But the village was still flooded, and Mei and Jia were stuck on the roof with only a little food left. They watched as the water flowed through the streets, carrying debris and tree branches with it.

Even though it was tough, the girls never gave up hope. They shared stories to keep each other's spirits up and watched the skies for any sign of rescuers. "We just have to keep waiting. Someone will come to help us," Mei told Jia, trying to stay brave.

The Rescue

On the third day, Mei and Jia heard the sound of a helicopter in the distance. They jumped up and waved their arms, trying to get the attention of the rescuers. Finally, the helicopter flew over their village and saw them on the rooftop. A rescue team quickly arrived by boat to help Mei and Jia off the roof and bring them to safety.

The girls were taken to a shelter where they were reunited with their families. Everyone was so proud of Mei and Jia for being brave and staying strong during such a scary time.

A Lesson in Courage and Friendship

Mei and Jia's survival during Typhoon Morakot is a story of courage, friendship, and never giving up hope. Even though they were scared and alone, the two friends supported each other and shared everything they had. Their teamwork and bravery helped them survive the dangerous flood until rescuers arrived.

For young readers, this story shows that courage means sticking together, helping each other, and staying hopeful, even in the toughest situations. Mei and Jia's experience during Typhoon Morakot is a powerful reminder that with friendship and determination, we can overcome any challenge.

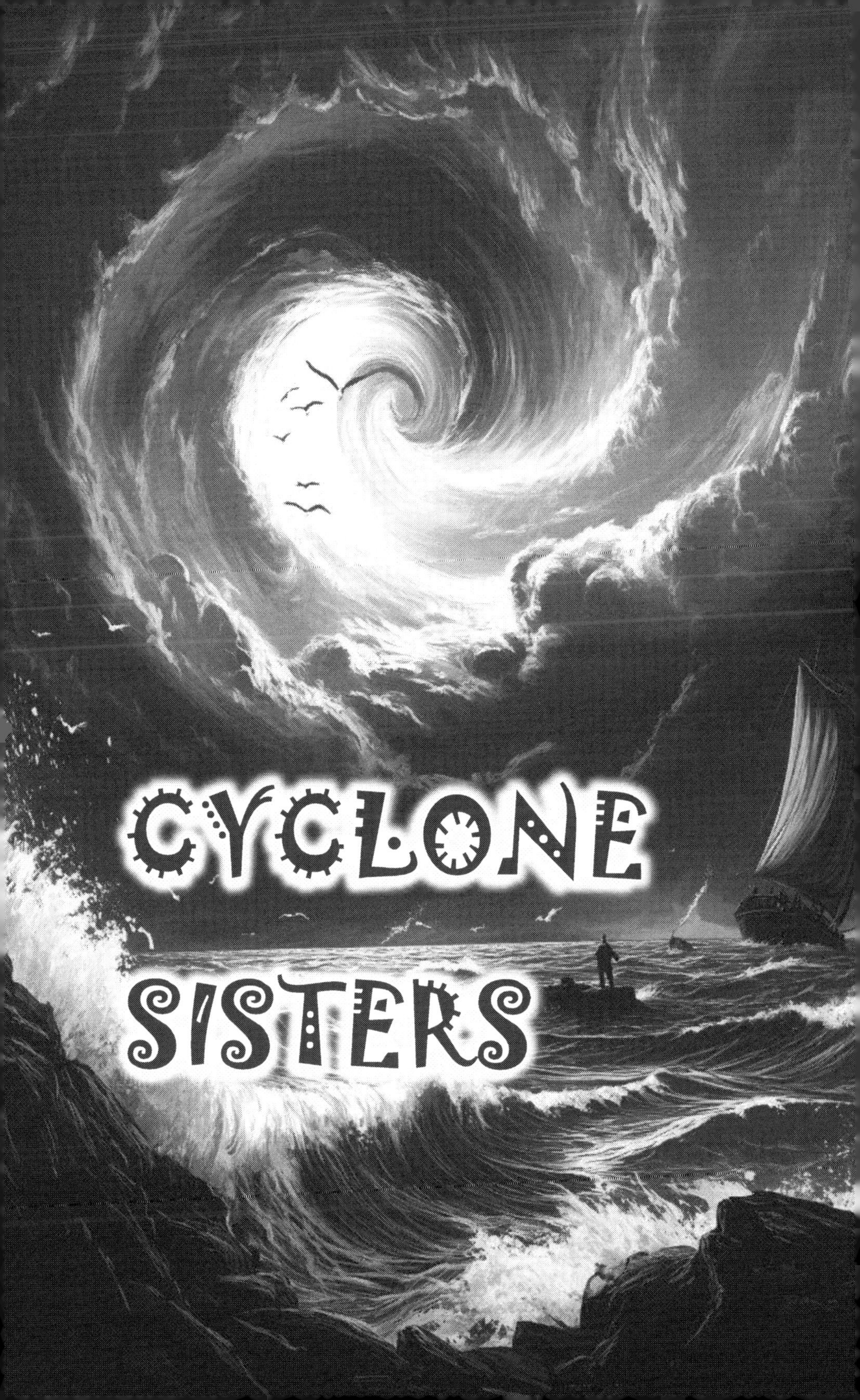
CYCLONE
SISTERS

13.1 What's a cyclone?

A cyclone is a huge, spinning storm that forms over the ocean. It has strong winds, and heavy rain, and can be very powerful. Cyclones are similar to hurricanes and typhoons, but they usually happen in different parts of the world, like Australia, India, and the South Pacific.

Let's find out how cyclones form, what happens during a cyclone, and why they can be dangerous.

How Do Cyclones Form?

1. **Warm Ocean Water**: Cyclones start over warm ocean waters. The heat from the water causes the air above it to rise.
2. **Rising Air**: As the warm air rises, cooler air rushes in to take its place, and the air begins to spin in a circle because of the Earth's rotation.
3. **Spinning Winds**: As the storm grows, the winds spin faster and faster around a calm center called the **eye**. The more it spins, the stronger the cyclone becomes.

What Happens During a Cyclone?

- **Strong Winds**: Cyclones have very strong winds that can blow as fast as a car on the highway! These winds can knock down trees, tear off roofs, and cause a lot of damage.
- **Heavy Rain**: Cyclones bring a lot of rain, which can cause flooding in towns and cities. The rain can last for days and make rivers and streets overflow with water.

- **Big Waves**: Cyclones also create big waves in the ocean, called **storm surges**. These waves can crash onto the shore and cause flooding along the coast.

Where Do Cyclones Happen?

Cyclones usually form in warm ocean waters near the equator, in places like the Indian Ocean, the South Pacific, and near Australia. In other parts of the world, like the Atlantic Ocean or the Pacific Ocean near Asia, similar storms are called **hurricanes** or **typhoons**, but they are all really the same type of storm.

How Can We Stay Safe During a Cyclone?

1. **Listen to Warnings**: Weather experts keep track of cyclones and give warnings when one is coming. If a cyclone is heading your way, it's important to listen to the news and follow the advice of local authorities.
2. **Stay Indoors**: The safest place to be during a cyclone is inside a strong building. Close all the windows and doors to protect yourself from the strong winds and rain.
3. **Be Prepared**: Before a cyclone comes, families should prepare by having food, water, and emergency supplies ready. It's important to have a plan in case the power goes out or if there's flooding.

Why Are Cyclones Dangerous?

Cyclones are dangerous because they bring strong winds, heavy rain, and big waves that can cause a lot of damage. The strong winds can blow away buildings, trees, and cars. The heavy rain can cause floods, and the big waves from the ocean can flood coastal areas. That's why it's important to be prepared and stay safe during a cyclone.

What Can We Learn?

Cyclones show us how powerful nature can be, but with the right knowledge and preparation, we can stay safe. By listening to weather warnings and taking shelter in safe places, people can protect themselves from the dangers of a cyclone.

13.2 Survival in Bangladesh

The Storm Arrives

In November 2007, a powerful storm called **Cyclone Sidr** was heading toward Bangladesh. Sisters Anika, who was 12, and her younger sister Farah, who was 8, lived in a small village with their family. The people in the village were preparing for the cyclone, which was predicted to be very strong, with heavy rain and strong winds.

As the storm got closer, the winds began to howl, and the rain poured down hard. The sisters were with their parents at home, but the storm grew so powerful that they were forced to leave and seek a safer place. In the confusion, Anika and Farah got separated from their family.

Finding Shelter

Anika knew they had to find shelter quickly. She remembered there was a **sturdy school building** nearby that was built to withstand storms. "Come on, Farah! We need to go to the school. It will keep us safe!" Anika said, holding her sister's hand tightly.

Even though Farah was scared, she trusted her big sister and followed her through the rain and wind. Together, they made their way to the school building, which stood strong against the storm. Other people from the village had also taken shelter there, and everyone was doing their best to stay calm.

Staying Strong Together

Inside the school, Anika and Farah found a corner where they could sit and wait out the storm. The wind was roaring outside, and they could hear things banging against the walls, but Anika stayed calm. She knew that it was important to stay brave for her little sister.

"Don't worry, Farah," Anika whispered. "This building is very strong, and we are safe here. The storm will pass soon." Farah hugged her sister tightly and nodded, finding comfort in Anika's words.

To keep their spirits up, Farah began to tell Anika stories about their family and things they would do once they were back home. Her optimism helped both of them feel a little less afraid, even though the storm outside was scary.

Waiting Out the Cyclone

The storm lasted for many hours, and it was hard to tell when it would end. The sisters shared the snacks they had brought and tried to rest, even though the noise outside made it difficult. Other people in the building also shared their food and blankets, and everyone worked together to keep each other safe and calm.

Anika kept a close eye on Farah, making sure she was warm and comfortable. Despite the frightening situation, she stayed strong and focused, knowing their parents would look for them once the storm was over.

The Storm Passes

Finally, the winds began to die down, and the rain stopped. People cautiously stepped outside to see the damage. The village was badly affected, with many homes destroyed and trees knocked over. But Anika and Farah were safe, and they were grateful to have found shelter in the school.

As they looked around, they spotted their parents in the crowd. With happy tears, they ran to their family and hugged them tightly. Their parents were so relieved to see them safe and sound.

A Lesson in Courage and Optimism

Anika and Farah's story during Cyclone Sidr shows us the power of **courage** and **optimism**. Even though they were scared and separated from their family, Anika's calm leadership and Farah's positive attitude helped them stay safe during the storm.

For young readers, this story reminds us that being brave doesn't mean you're not afraid. It means staying calm and helping others, even when things are tough. Anika and Farah's experience during Cyclone Sidr teaches us that with courage, trust, and hope, we can face any challenge and come through stronger.

Chapter 14: CONCLUSION

As we come to the end of *Natural Disasters*, we've traveled through some of the most powerful and awe-inspiring forces on Earth. Through each story, we've seen how friendship, courage, and quick thinking can make all the difference when faced with natural disasters. From massive earthquakes and towering tsunamis to fierce hurricanes and sandstorms, these young heroes showed us that even in the most challenging situations, we can find hope and strength within ourselves and in those around us.

Each story in this book reveals that you don't have to be a superhero to make a difference. The courage to help a friend, the wisdom to follow safety rules, and the teamwork to stick together - these are qualities that each one of us can develop. The young heroes we met showed that by staying calm, using what they knew, and supporting each other, they could overcome even the toughest obstacles.

For you, young reader, remember that true courage doesn't mean you're never afraid. It means doing what's right even when you are afraid. By learning from these incredible stories, you now know that you, too, can be prepared, stay safe, and help others. And who knows? Someday, you might be the one to inspire others with your own story of courage and resilience.

So, as you close this book, keep these lessons close to your heart. You have the power to be brave, help others, and face challenges with confidence. Always believe in yourself, and never forget that with a strong spirit and a caring heart, you can make it through anything that comes your way.

INDEX

BONUS 1: AMAZING FACTS

1-20: Earthquakes

1. The largest earthquake ever recorded was in Chile in 1960, measuring a whopping 9.5 on the Richter scale.

2. The planet experiences an estimated 500,000 earthquakes every year, but most are too small to be felt.

3. Japan has more earthquakes than any other country, earning it the nickname "the Land of Quakes."

4. Earthquakes can make the ground ripple like waves in the ocean!

5. In 1985, a 9-year-old girl invented a device to predict small tremors after living through an earthquake in Mexico City.

6. Some animals, like dogs and elephants, are believed to sense earthquakes before they happen.

7. The Earth's crust is like a giant puzzle, made up of tectonic plates that move a few centimeters every year.

8. The San Andreas Fault in California can cause massive earthquakes and has inspired several disaster movies.

9. Earthquakes can cause the ground to liquefy, making solid soil behave like quicksand.

10. Seismometers, the devices used to measure earthquakes, can detect underground nuclear tests.

11. The word "tsunami" comes from the Japanese words "tsu" (harbor) and "nami" (wave).

12. The 1906 San Francisco earthquake caused so many fires that the city burned for days.

13. An earthquake in China in 1556 is believed to have killed over 830,000 people, making it the deadliest ever recorded.

14. Sometimes earthquakes cause earthquake lights, and mysterious glowing skies are reported during major quakes.

15. The longest recorded earthquake lasted 10 minutes, striking Sumatra in 2004.

16. Some earthquakes happen deep within the Earth, up to 400 miles below the surface!

17. Aftershocks can last for weeks or even months after a big earthquake.

18. Earthquake-proof buildings sway like trees to survive strong tremors.

19. Earthquakes on Mars, called "marsquakes," have been detected by NASA rovers.

20. The moon also experiences quakes, known as moonquakes, caused by meteor impacts or lunar tidal forces.

21–40: Volcanoes

21. Mount Vesuvius buried the Roman city of Pompeii in ash in 79 AD, preserving it for thousands of years.

22. The loudest sound in recorded history came from the eruption of Krakatoa in 1883, heard over 3,000 miles away.

23. The word "volcano" comes from the Roman god of fire, Vulcan.

24. Lava from Kīlauea in Hawaii can move as fast as 40 mph!

25. Supervolcanoes, like Yellowstone, could erupt with enough force to affect the entire planet.

26. Iceland sits on two tectonic plates, making it one of the most volcanic places on Earth.

27. The ash cloud from Mount Tambora's eruption in 1815 caused the "Year Without a Summer."

28. Some volcanoes erupt underwater, creating new islands.

29. Volcanic lightning happens when ash and rock particles rub together, creating an electrical charge.

30. The most active volcano in the world is Mount Etna in Italy, which has been erupting for over 3,500 years.

31. Lava flows can reach temperatures of up to 1,250 degrees Fahrenheit (677 degrees Celsius).

32. The volcanic eruption on La Palma in 2021 created rivers of lava that reached the sea.

33. Mauna Loa in Hawaii is the largest volcano on Earth, spanning over 5,271 square kilometers.

34. Some people live near volcanoes because the ash makes the soil very fertile for farming.

35. Volcanic eruptions can cause acid rain, which damages crops and ecosystems.

36. A supervolcanic eruption 74,000 years ago nearly wiped out early humans.

37. There are about 1,500 active volcanoes on Earth today.

38. Pele's Hair is a type of volcanic glass that forms thin strands, named after the Hawaiian goddess of fire.

39. Some volcanic eruptions cause lava fountains that shoot magma hundreds of feet into the air.

40. Mount Erebus in Antarctica is one of the few volcanoes with a permanent lava lake.

41–60: Hurricanes, Typhoons, and Cyclones

41. Hurricanes are called typhoons in Asia and cyclones in Australia.

42. The center of a hurricane, called the eye, is surprisingly calm and peaceful.

43. The largest hurricane ever recorded, Hurricane Patricia, had winds of 215 mph!

44. Hurricane names are retired if the storm is especially deadly or costly.

45. Hurricanes can produce over 2 trillion gallons of rain per day.

46. The deadliest hurricane in U.S. history, the 1900 Galveston Hurricane, killed over 6,000 people.

47. Hurricane winds can spawn tornadoes, creating double trouble for areas in their path.

48. Hurricanes are powered by warm ocean water, which fuels their growth.

49. Storm surges, or walls of water pushed by hurricane winds, cause the most destruction during these storms.

50. The term "hurricane" comes from Huracán, the Mayan god of wind and storms.

51. Cyclone Tracy in 1974 was so strong it nearly wiped out the city of Darwin, Australia.

52. Hurricane Sandy was nicknamed "Frankenstorm" because it hit the U.S. around Halloween.

53. Hurricanes can cause fish to rain when they suck up water from the ocean.

54. The Saffir-Simpson scale measures hurricanes from Category 1 to Category 5, based on wind speeds.

55. Hurricanes can grow as wide as 500 miles, covering entire regions.

56. Hurricane hunters are brave scientists who fly planes into storms to study them.

57. In 1992, Hurricane Andrew left thousands of iguanas stranded after the storm tore through Florida.

58. Hurricanes can last for weeks if conditions remain favorable.

59. Hurricane eyewalls are the most dangerous part of the storm, with the strongest winds and rain.

60. Some of Jupiter's storms are so massive they could fit multiple Earths inside them.

61–80: Tornadoes

61. The fastest wind speed ever recorded was in a tornado: 318 mph in Oklahoma in 1999.

62. Tornadoes are also called twisters or cyclones, depending on where you live.

63. The United States has the most tornadoes, especially in an area called Tornado Alley.

64. The largest tornado ever recorded, the El Reno tornado, was over 2.6 miles wide.

65. Tornadoes can form over water, creating waterspouts.

66. Tornado sirens were originally used during World War II to warn of air raids.

67. Tornadoes can lift cars, trees, and even houses into the air.

68. The "Wizard of Oz" tornado scene is one of the most famous depictions of a twister in popular culture.

69. Tornadoes are rated on the Enhanced Fujita Scale, from EF0 to EF5.

70. An average tornado travels at about 30 mph, but some can reach 70 mph!

71. Tornadoes form from rotating storm clouds called supercells.

72. Tornadoes can leave behind debris trails stretching for miles.

73. The safest place during a tornado is an underground shelter or basement.

74. Tornadoes have been spotted on every continent, except Antarctica.

75. In 1925, the Tri-State Tornado traveled over 219 miles across three states.

76. Some tornadoes are nearly invisible, only visible because of the debris they carry.

77. Tornadoes can last from a few seconds to over an hour.

78. Dust devils, small spinning air columns, are like mini-tornadoes and harmless in comparison.

79. Tornadoes can suck up frogs and fish, leading to bizarre "animal rain."

80. Some people chase tornadoes for science—or for fun!

81–100: Tsunamis, Floods, and More

81. Tsunamis can travel as fast as a jet plane, up to 500 mph in open water.

82. The tallest tsunami wave ever recorded was 1,720 feet, in Alaska's Lituya Bay in 1958.

83. The 2004 Indian Ocean tsunami affected 14 countries and caused massive devastation.

84. Floods are the most common natural disaster worldwide.

85. In deserts, sudden flash floods can occur even if it hasn't rained nearby.

86. Tsunamis are caused by undersea earthquakes, landslides, or volcanic eruptions.

87. Flood plains, while risky, often have fertile soil, making them attractive for farming.

88. Some ancient cities were abandoned due to constant flooding.

89. Dams are built to control floods but can fail under extreme pressure.

90. The Great Mississippi Flood of 1927 was one of the worst in U.S. history.

91. Ice jams can cause floods when chunks of ice block rivers.

92. Fire tornadoes, or "firenadoes," occur during wildfires with strong winds.

93. The 1902 eruption of Mount Pelée sent a cloud of hot gas racing down, destroying an entire city in minutes.

94. Blizzards can create snowdrifts tall enough to bury entire houses.

95. Landslides can move millions of tons of earth in seconds.

96. The Dead Sea flood over 4,000 years ago may have inspired flood myths like Noah's Ark.

97. Hailstones can grow as large as a baseball during severe storms.

98. The Sahara Desert can experience sudden floods after rare rains.

99. A volcanic eruption in Iceland in 2010 caused ash clouds that disrupted air travel across Europe.

100. The Great Chicago Fire of 1871 may have started when a cow knocked over a lantern.

BONUS 2: KNOWLEDGE QUIZ

1. What causes an earthquake?
a) Heavy rain
b) Movement of the Earth's plates
c) Strong winds
d) Large ocean waves

2. Which natural disaster is a huge wave caused by an underwater earthquake?
a) Tornado
b) Typhoon
c) Tsunami
d) Cyclone

3. What is the calm center of a hurricane called?
a) The Eye
b) The Heart
c) The Core
d) The Storm

4. During a flood, what should you avoid walking through?
a) Tall grass
b) Deep water
c) Sand dunes
d) Rocky trails

6. What is a wildfire?
a) A fire in a desert
b) A fire that spreads quickly in forests or grasslands
c) A controlled campfire
d) A volcanic eruption

6. What is the opening at the top of a volcano where lava flows out called?
a) Crater
b) Pit
c) Basin
d) Valley

7. Which natural disaster involves strong winds and heavy snow?
a) Wildfire
b) Hurricane
c) Snowstorm
d) Avalanche

8. In which natural disaster does a large amount of snow suddenly slide down a mountain?
a) Cyclone
b) Avalanche
c) Snowstorm
d) Flood

9. What's the difference between a typhoon and a cyclone?
a) Cyclones only happen in the mountains
b) Typhoons happen in the Pacific Ocean, while cyclones occur in other areas like the Indian Ocean
c) Cyclones are caused by earthquakes
d) Typhoons don't have strong winds

10. What type of natural disaster is caused by extreme heat and dry conditions?
a) Wildfire
b) Earthquake
c) Flood

d) Snowstorm

11. What is one of the main causes of a flood?
a) Excessive sunlight
b) Strong winds
c) Too much rain
d) Earthquakes

12. What should you do if you are outside during a sandstorm?
a) Stand tall and face the wind
b) Run as fast as you can
c) Seek shelter and cover your mouth and nose
d) Jump up and down to stay warm

13. Which country is known as the "Land of Quakes"?
a) Indonesia
b) Japan
c) Chile
d) New Zealand

14. What caused the loudest sound in recorded history?
a) An earthquake in Chile
b) The eruption of Krakatoa in 1883
c) A meteor impact in Siberia
d) A volcanic eruption in Iceland

15. Where is Tornado Alley located?
a) In South America
b) In Europe
c) In Southeast Asia
d) In the United States

16. What should you do if caught in a tsunami?

a) Run to a tall building or higher ground
b) Stay near the shoreline to monitor waves
c) Lie flat on the beach
d) Try to outswim the waves

17. What was the largest earthquake ever recorded?
a) The 1906 San Francisco earthquake
b) The 2011 Japan earthquake
c) The 1960 Chile earthquake
d) The 2004 Sumatra earthquake

18. How many earthquakes happen around the world each year?
a) 50,000
b) 100,000
c) 500,000
d) 1,000,000

ANSWERS

1. b) Movement of the Earth's plates
2. c) Tsunami
3. a) The Eye
4. b) Deepwater
5. b) A fire that spreads quickly in forests or grasslands
6. a) Crater
7. c) Snowstorm
8. b) Avalanche
9. b) Typhoons happen in the Pacific Ocean, while cyclones occur in other areas like the Indian Ocean
10. a) Wildfire
11. c) Too much rain
12. c) Seek shelter and cover your mouth and nose
13. b) Japan
14. b) The eruption of Krakatoa in 1883
15. d) In the United States
16. a) Run to a tall building or higher ground
17. c) The 1960 Chile earthquake
18. c) 500,000

Made in the USA
Las Vegas, NV
19 December 2024

4a3bd711-5d9d-473a-b164-f3dd4144b734R01